# CONTENTS

# MODERN ESSAYS & LETTERS For Junior Classes

*Compiled by:*
**G. Jain** *(M.A. Eng.)*

NEW DELHI (INDIA)

MODERN
# ESSAYS & LETTERS



*Published by*

*An Imprint of*

**MAANU GRAPHICS**
**(PUBLISHERS OF GENERAL BOOKS)**
5FF, Ganpati Bhawan, 21 Ansari Road,
Darya Ganj, New Delhi-110002
Ph: 65285220, 64138266
E-mail : maanugraphics@yahoo.com



*Printed at*
NEW Z. A. Printers, Delhi

# ESSAYS

## MAHATMA GANDHI

Mahatma Gandhi has been the greatest man of modern times. He is respected by the whole world. When he was killed, the whole world wept. He was the Father of the Nation.

People called him Bapu (father) in love. His full name was Mohan Das Karam Chand Gandhi. Gandhiji was born in the middle class family of Porbandar on 2nd October, 1869.

His early education was in Gujarat. He went to school at the age of seven. He was married to Kasturba at the age of thirteen. Later he went to England to study law and become a barrister and started practice in Bombay. But he was not successful as a lawyer.

He went to Africa. There he fought for the rights of Indians. On his return to India, he joined Congress.

Soon he became an important leader of the Congress. Then he started non-cooperation movement against the British rule in India.

He was a great devotee of ahinsa or non-violence. He was sent to jail many times. At last India won freedom on 15th August, 1947 under his prompt leadership.

Gandhiji was a saint-politician. His faith in God was firm and deep. He never told a lie. He advised people never to utter untruth. He was a great social reformer.

He was killed on 30th January 1948. He died in the cause of Hindu Muslim unity. His Samadhi at Rajghat is visited by hundreds of people daily.

## INDIRA GANDHI

Indira Gandhi was born on November 19, 1917 in her grandfather's house in Allahabad, in northern India. Shewas the daughter of Pandit Jawaharlal Nehru. Her mother's name was Kamala Nehru.

In 1942 Indira and Feroze were married. In 1947 Indira became her father's hostess as he leads India. Her upbringing had taught her much about freedom and struggle.

Now, at her father's side she was to gain an education into the workings of a democracy and the realities of power. In 1959 she became congress president.

In 1964 her father died, his successor was Lal Bhadur Shartri. Mr. Shartri died after two years in office. On

Shastri's death, she was elected the first woman Prime Minister of the country. She led the country for sixteen years.

In 1971, she gave crushing defeat to Pakistan. She nationalised the Banks and abolished the Privy Purse. These two steps made her the champion of the poor.

Her life was part of the story of modern India. She was killed by two of her bodyguards. She was sixty-four years old. She was a lady of rare qualities.

No one ever doubted the courage of the remarkable woman who had sometimes been called "The Devi of India" and no one ever doubted that with her death a chapter of India's history ended.

## SUBHASH CHANDRA BOSE

Netaji Subhash Chandra was born on January 23rd 1897 in Orissa as the ninth child among fourteen, of Janakinath Bose and Prabhavati devi. His father was a famous Lawyer.

He was strongly influenced by Swami Vivekananda's teachings and was known for his patriotic zeal as a student. He believed in violence. After passing B.A., he went to England.

In England he appeared for the Indian Civil Service competitive examination in 1920, and came out fourth in order of merit.

However, Subhas Chandra Bose was deeply disturbed by the Jallianwalla Bagh massacre, and left his Civil Services apprenticeship midway to return to India in 1921. Subhash joined the Congress movement. He was elected President of the Congress in 1939.

At the time of World War II, the British were in a tight spot due to the pressure from Hitler. Netaji was under detention in Calcutta at that time, and decided to take advantage of the situation.

Subhash went to Germany. Here he approached Hitler with his cause. Hitler was impressed and promised to help him. Netaji then organized all the Indian Prisoners of War to form the Liberation Army and the Indian National Army.

1945 witnessed the I.N.A. waging a war from the North - Eest of our country. He inspired his army with the battle cry 'Delhi Chalo'.

Even though he did not succeed in this battle, he had driven home his message. The Britishers realised that the Indians were serious about gaining independence, and would assume any means towards that end.

On August 17, 1945, Bose died in a plane crash while flying from Bangkok to Tokyo. He did not live to see the Indian Independence, but his spirit still lives through his words - JAI HIND.

# RABINDRANATH TAGORE

Rabindranath Tagore was born in 1861. He was the youngest son of Debendranath Tagore. He was educated at home; and although at seventeen he was sent to England for formal schooling, he did not finish his studies there.

He also started an experimental school at Shantiniketan where he tried his Upanishadic ideals of education.

Tagore was knighted by the ruling British Government in 1915, but within a few years he resigned the honour as a protest against British policies in India.

Tagore had early success as a writer in his native Bengal. With his translations of some of his poems he became rapidly known in the West.

For the world he became the voice of India's spiritual heritage; and for India, especially for Bengal, he became a great living institution.

He wrote musical dramas, dance dramas, essays of all types, travel diaries, and two autobiographies, one in his middle years and the other shortly before his death in 1941.

Tagore also left numerous drawings and paintings, and songs for which he wrote the music himself.

# LOKMANYA BAL GANGADHAR TILAK

Bal Gangadhar Tilak on born July 22, 1856 at Ratnagiri. He was from a royal family, but his father was a school teacher.

He did his schooling from Poona High School and then joined the Deccan College. He completed a degree in law in 1879.

He was one of the prime architects of modern India and heralded Asian nationalism. His philosophy could not survive after his death as India came under sway of Mahatma Gandhi.

Tilak joined the other freedom fighters in their struggle for independence. He believed that the British had to be paid back in their own coin by fighting back.

In 1881, Tilak started two magazines, 'Kesari' in Marathi and 'Maratha' in English. In 1885, he established the Deccan Education Society.

Tilak gave the famous slogan, "Swaraj is my birthright, and I shall have it." In 1905, Tilak was arrested and sent to Mandalay Jail for six years.

He started the Home Rule Movement. Tilak is known as the Father of Indian Nationalism. He died on 1st May, 1920.

# MOTHER TERESA

Mother Teresa was born in Yugoslavia on 26th August 1910. She became a nun at the age of 18. She came to India as a Loretto sister to teach in Loretto convents in Kolkata.

In 1950 she started the famous order of the 'Missionaries of Charity'. Soon many homes for the homeless, schools and hospitals were opened all over the country and abroad.

For her great work of selfless love for the unloved she had been awarded many prizes and titles both in India and in other countries. She was too big a person for these awards.

The holy work she did could never be made small by being paid for. She worked untiringly till the day she passed away. She died on the 5th of September, 1997 in Kolkata.

She was a real saint and both Kolkata and India are proud that she died as an Indian. In her death India lost an angel of mercy that day.

It was indeed a black Friday for the whole world. The work she started carries on without any lack of love by her followers all over the world.

# SARDAR VALLABHBHAI PATEL

Sardar Vallabhbhai Patel was born on 31 October, 1875, in a farmer's family in Nadiad, Gujarat.

His father, Zaverbhai, had served in the army of Jhansi ki Rani, and his mother, Ladbai, was a deeply religious woman. Vallabhbhai's initial schooling was in Gujarati.

After his schooling, he went to England for higher studies. In 1913 after studying law there he returned back to India as a barrister.

Vallabhbhai was married to Zaverbai in 1891. The couple had two children-a daughter Maniben, born in April of 1904, and a son Dayabhai, born in November of 1905. Zaverbai died in January of 1909.

Patel came into touch with Gandhi and gave up his practice. Vallabhbhai was deeply influenced by Gandhiji. The title of 'Sardar' was given to him by Gandhiji. In 1918, he entered politics.

In 1931, he became the President three years as he was the leader of the Quit India Movement.

In 1947, India became independent and Vallabhbhai became the Home Minister of Independent India.

His service to the nation will always be remembered. He died in the year 1949. He was known as the Iron Man of India.

## LAL BAHADUR SHASTRI

Lal Bahadur Shastri was born on 2nd October, 1904 at Mughal Sarai town in Uttar Pradesh. His father Sharda Prasad was a man of very limited means.

He was hardly two years old when he lost his father. After his father's death, his mother left for her parent's house.

After receiving primary education at Mughal Sarai, he went to his uncle at Varanasi and joined Harish Chander High School.

Thereafter he joined Kashi Vidya Peeth at Varanasi and passed his examinations in the first division.

He offered Satyagraha and was sentenced to imprisonment at different times. In all he had to spend almost eight long years in internment.

As prime minister he had to face a multitude of problems. In fact, he assumed the office of Prime Minister immediately after the death of Jawahar Lal Nehru.

During Indo-Pak war, Lal Bahadur Shastri showed rare quality of courage and determination. His speeches during the war inspired the people of India.

They were galvanised. He gave a slogan "Jai Jawan Jai Kissan". The slogan instilled in the forces a triumphant spirit.

He died on 11th Jan, 1966. The tragic news of his death at Tashkant spread-like a wild fire. Now Vijayghat stands memorial to this heroic man.

Lal Bahadur Shastri was truly a great man who gave less importance to himself and more to institutions.

## ASHOKA - THE GREAT

One of the greatest rulers of India's history is Ashoka. He was born in the year 304 B.C. After the death of his father, Ashoka became the king of Pataliputra. He was a very good king.

Ashoka had already gained experience of administration during his father's rule. Eight years after he took his throne, Ashoka's powerful armies attacked and conquered Kalinga.

Although he had conquered many other places, this violent war was the last war he ever fought and a turning point of his career. He was disgusted by the extreme deaths of numerous civilians, especially the Brahmans.

In the nineteenth century, a large number of edicts written in Brahmi script carved on rocks and stone pillars were discovered in India, proving the existence of Ashoka.

Ashoka died in the thirty-eighth year of his reign, 232 B.C. The Buddhist ideas no longer inspire the government and at the same time, his descendents quarrel over the successions.

In less than fifty years after his death, the Maurya Empire collapsed and fell into pieces.

## GOPAL KRISHNA GOKHALE

Gopal Krishna Gokhale was born on 9th March, 1866. He was one of the greatest freedom fighters of India.

Hc finished his schooling in 1881 and graduated from Mumbai University in 1884. He was the Principal of Fergusson College, Pune.

Gokhale had a very good memory. He became a follower of Justice Ranade. He was very truthful in his work. Gandhiji considered Gokhale as his political guru.

In 1905, Gokhale became the President of the Congress. Gopal Krishna Gokhale served the country faithfully.

But his health did not support him for long. He passed away on 19 th February, 1915 and India lost a great patriot.

## PANDIT JAWAHAR LAL NEHRU

Pandit Jawaharlal Nehru was born on 14th November, 1889. He was born in Allahabad. Moti Lal Nehru was his father. He was a great lawyer.

Jawaharlal Nehru got his early education at home. The he went to England for higher studies. He returned to India in 1912. Later he became a lawyer.

He gave up his practice and joined the freedom movement under Mahatma Gandhi. He was totally involved in India's freedom movement.

He was sent to jail several times. In 1947 when India became free, he was elected the first Prime Minister.

He was a great statesman, idealist and a dreamer. He has written many books. He worked hard to serve his country.

Pandit Nehru loved children. And the children called him Chacha Nehru with love. He always liked and enjoyed the company of children. He always wore a rose in his dress. His birthday is now celebrated as Children's Day.

India made great progress under his leadership. He died on 27th May, 1964. He was one of the builders of modern India. We always remember him fondly.

## MIRA BAI

Mira was a queen of Rajasthan who is known more for her devotion than her political position. There are so many stories about Mira Bai that it is very difficult to tell the facts of her life from legend.

She was born about 1500 and was married at the age of 13. From an early age she showed more interest in religious devotions than to her worldly responsibilities.

It is said that she neglected her marital responsibilities. When queried about it, she said that it was impossible for her to be married to the king when she was already married to Krishna.

A major change in her life occurred at the time of the death of her husband. It was customary in those days for a wife to commit satti.

Satti is the self immolation upon the husband's funeral pyre. She refused to comply, whereupon her in-laws began harassing her.

She then left the palace and began wandering throughout Rajasthan, preaching and gaining followers.

Mira is known for the many bhajans that she left behind. These bhajans are in praise of lord Krishna and held in great esteem for their high literary value.

She is believed to have died around 1550.

## MY CLASS TEACHER

I read in standard VII. Miss Sarita Verma is my class teacher. She is an M.A., M.Ed. She is an experienced teacher. She is an ideal teacher.

She is a charming lady. She is stout. She is of fair colour. She teaches us English and Music. She makes her lesson interesting.

She never gets irritated when students ask her their doubts. She explains again and again. She is about 27 years of age. She is always cheerful.

She is a nice teacher. She never gets angry when a student fails to learn. She encourages him or her to learn again and again. She explains things in simple and clear manner. She is gentle and soft-spoken.

She is always ready to help her pupils. But she is very strict in discipline. She always wants us to be disciplined and tidy.

I am glad that Miss Sarita Verma is my class-teacher. She makes her teaching interesting with the help of charts, maps, or toys. Sometimes she takes us on a visit to some interesting place.

She is very simple. Due to her good qualities students always praise her and hold her in high esteem. I always take care to do well in the class and try to be like her. I am proud of my class teacher.

## MY NEIGHBOUR

Blessed are those who have good neighbours, I am lucky to have Mr. Sunil as my next door neighbour. He is every inch a gentleman. He is very helpful to all.

Mr. Sunil is a wealthy businessman. He is very intelligent. He has two pet dogs. In spite of being rich he is not arrogant. He speaks to every one and is generous and kind.

Mr. Sunil has four children—two sons and two daughters. The eldest son helps him in the business. The second son is of my age and studies in a public school. His daughters are students of class nine and seven.

All the members of his family are good. His father is very kind and religious. His children are good natured and have good manners. They are good at studies too.

We mix freely with them. Sometimes Mr. Sunil gives us a lift in his car. We exchange sweets and presents with them on festivals.

Mr. Sunil and the members of his family are very cooperative and helpful. They have forged a kind of family feeling among the neighbours.

## MY MOTHERLAND

India is my country. It is a country of villages. Most people live in the villages than in the cities. There are big cities like Mumbai and Delhi.

The Himalayas, the highest mountain in the world, are in the north. There are many rivers but Ganga is the longest.

We have set up big industries and built dams. We grow several kinds of crops too. India is known for its lions, elephants and tigers.

The peacock is the national bird of India. It is a country of great saints and sages. She has given birth to scholars like C.V. Raman, Ravinder Nath Tagore, Dr. J.C. Bose and Dr. Homi Bhabha.

The land of Upnishads, Mahabharata, and Ramayana has been the cradle of ancient civilization. Leaders like Mahatma Gandhi, Subhash Chandra Bose and Sardar Patel got her freedom.

Since then our country has been making steady progress in the field of agriculture, education, medicine, science and industry. Today, we are self-sufficient in almost every sphere of life.

## MY HOBBY

A hobby is an interesting thing. It gives great joy. It makes life lively. It is something done in spare time. It is not done for money.

Kite-flying is my hobby. I like it very much. I have a good collection of kites. There are kites of many shapes and sizes. They are of many colours.

Kites are made of thin paper and bamboo strips, A special string is used in flying-kites. It is a popular hobby. Kite-flying matches are held at the sea-beach.

On Sundays I fly kites. I do it from the top-roof of my house. It is very delightful to see kites flying in the clear, blue sky. It soothes our eyes.

Sometimes I go to the river-front with my friends. There we enjoy kite-flying. Many elderly people also come there. They are skilled kite-fliers.

Gardening is my another hobby. There is a beautiful garden in my house. I have divided this garden into two parts.

In one part I grow flowers of different varieties. I look after the plants and water them daily.

I keep the spot neat and clean. I have four plants of tomatoes in my garden. Daily I pluck two or three tomatoes and eat them raw. They are very tasty.

My garden is very useful to me. I use my pocket-money for my hobbies.

## MY SCHOOL

I study in Jain Happy School in Daryaganj. It is a double-storeyed building. Its clock-tower can be seen from very far.

There are thirty rooms. All the rooms are spacious and well ventilated. There is a big library, a science laboratory, and one office room in my school.

Our library has thousands of books. There are many magazines. Students may be seen reading there in the hall.

There is a large playground. It also has a beautiful garden. There are many kinds of plants and trees. My school is one of the best schools in my city.

My school has 40 teachers and a principal. All our teachers are highly qualified. Our Principal is a middle-aged gentleman.

He believes in simple living and high thinking. He never punishes a student. About a thousand students come to study in my school.

I love my school very much. I am proud of my school.

## MY CLASS ROOM

I read in D.A.V. Public Senior Secondary School. It has two storey building. I read in V class. My class sits at the first floor. Our classroom is very neat and clean.

There are twenty girls and ten boys in our class. There are thirty-five desks and chairs. Each student has a chair and a desk. Every desk has a shelf. We keep our books in the shelf.

Our class-room is very big. Two electric fans hang from the ceiling. There are two electric tubes also.

The walls are white and clean. They are decorated with picture charts and maps. There is also one almirah in one corner of the class-room.

The teacher sits in the chair facing the students. The students are well-mannered. Teachers teach well.

They are good and kind to the students. They love us like their own children.

## MY FIRST DAY AT SCHOOL

I had sought admission in DAV Public School. I got up early in the morning and got myself prepared.

I boarded the school bus and reached the school. The sight of the grand building made me nervous.

I entered the main gate. Many boys were sitting there in a group. They welcomed me in a good manner.

One of the boys befriended me. He took me to the class-room. He introduced me to other boys. I took my seat in the first row. Then there was teaching for four periods.

During recess period, we rushed out of the class. I was, alone in the play-ground. Finding me alone, some boys approached me. They cut silly jokes but I was not annoyed.

They got pleased with my nature and took me round the school building. They also showed me the Library. They also made me share their lunch packets.

Again there was teaching for four periods. Two boys visited my house when the school was over.

## MY GRAND MOTHER

My grand mother is very dear to me. She is an old woman. My grand mother's name is Mrs. Santosh Gupta.

She is sixty-five years old. Even at this age she is very active. She takes care of my every need.

She gets up early in the morning. She is a religious lady. Her hair is white as snow. She is tall and thin. She wears clean and loose clothes.

She is very nice lady. She is old but dear to everybody. She supervises all important jobs in the family. She is simple in every way. She eats very little food.

My parents seek her advice in all matters. She likes to see religious films. She is always seen praying to God.

At night, she tells me stories. She also asks me to pay attention to my studies. She loves me very much. I love her very much. May she live long and make my life comfortable!

## MY FAMILY

I come of a noble family. My family is small. My family is well-known in the city. There are five members in my family, my grand mother, my parents, my sister and I.

I am the eldest son of my parents. My sister is younger than me. My sister's name geeta.

Geeta and I go to the same school. She is in the second grade. She love me very much. I also love her.

My father is a teacher. He is a tall man. His age is 42 years. My mother is a housewife. She is 40 years old.

She loves me very much. She looks after my needs well. My parents are loving and kind.

My grandmother is an old lady. She is 75 years old. She tells us tales at night. Ours is a small but happy family.

All our neighbours love us. We are peace-loving people and never fight with the neighbours. My family is a very happy family.

## MY MOTHER

Radha Aggarwal is my mother. She is a kind lady. She is very good in her behaviour. Everybody in the family likes her. She has many qualities of head and heart.

She is highly educated and intelligent. She is very hard-working, kind, caring and loving. Her love for us has no limits.

She is a housewife and ever busy. She gets up earlier than others and goes to bed last of all.

She cooks food, washes our clothes, looks after our every need and comfort. She enjoys serving us. Sometimes, I feel sorry for her and help her in her work in my own humble way.

Her love and care are a great source of inspiration to me. They help me in keeping good health and be cheerful.

It is because of her that I am so good at studies. If I am ill, she would leave no stone unturned to look after me till I get well and healthy.

She prepares many delicious dishes for us. We can never forget her service and sacrifices. She is really great, wonderful, loving and kind.

If my mother falls ill, there is disorder in the house. Everybody is then ill at ease. It is like a disaster for all of us. We always pray for her health and happiness. My mother is really a jewel.

## MYSELF

I am a boy. I am twelve-year-old. My name is Pankaj. My grandfather gave me this name. All the members of our family are well educated.

I live in Delhi. It is a beautiful city. It is the capital of India. My mother is a housewife and my father a serviceman.

My parents are very kind. I have a brother and a sister. My brother is younger to me by eight years, but my sister, Jyoti, is older to me.

Mahesh, Rupesh, Pinky and Hema are my cousin brothers and sisters.

My brother's name is Ashok. We live in our own house. It is beautiful with big lawn and a small garden.

I go to school in bus. It is about 5 kms. away from my house. My brother and sister also study in the same school.

It is a govt. model school. I am good at studies. I learn many things in the school. We also play games.

I havc many friends. But Rahul is my best friend. He is my class-fellow. He is pretty and intelligent.

Some times he comes to my house. I also visit his house on holidays. His mother is a teacher. His father is doctor.

When I grow up. I want to become a teacher. This is my first and last wish to teach the students.

## MY PARENTS

Child is known by his family. I come of a noble family. Shri Mr. Rakesh Gupta is my father. He is a teacher in a Government School.

He gives special attention to poor and weak students. So all the students respect him. He is about fifty.

He helps every one. He helps me in my studies. He loves me very much.

Mrs. Rita Gupta is my mother. She is a noble lady. She is forty-five years old. She is a teacher. She is very hard working lady. She keeps the house neat and clean.

She gets up early in the morning. She gives bed tea to my father early in the morning. She prepares breakfast for all of us. She teaches well in the school. Her students lover her very much.

She wears a sari. She makes me ready for school. She helps me in my studies also. She keeps the house neat and clean. She loves me very much. In short, I am proud of my parents.

## MY PET DOG

Dogs have often been called "Man's best friend". The dog is a familiar animal. It is very useful. I have a dog as a pet. This seems very true about my dog Roki.

Roki and I go for a walk every morning because he has to ease himself. He socializes a lot with the passers by. At times he barks at people whom he does not particularly like.

Roki barks whenever it sees a stranger or a thief. I feel terrible whenever Roki falls ill. He becomes as helpless as a baby during any sickness.

With Roki around I never feel lonely. Holidays are great because Roki and I spend a lot of time running and playing in the park with a ball or with a bone.

I feed Roki every day and I love to make his meals because he enjoys eating and I love to watch him licking his plate dry within minutes.

Roki is my pet and I can easily say that he is the best friend that I have.

## MY BEST FRIEND

I have many friends at school. I like all of them. But Neru is my best friend. She is my classmate and neighbour. She comes of a respectable family. She never loses her temper.

Her father is a doctor and her mother is a teacher. We both read in IV class. We go to school together. We sit on the same desk.

Neru is ten years old. She is good and nice girl. She is strong and healthy. She rises early in the morning.

She is very regular in her daily routine. She cleans her teeth everyday. She takes bath daily. She wears simple clothes. Her dress is always clean.

We read together. She always helps me in studies. She always stands first in the class. She is the monitor of our class. She is a good student. She is honest and simple. She does not waste her time in idle talks.

She is very simple girl. She wins prizes every year. She obeys her parents and teachers. She come to my house everyday. She comes from a noble family. We play and read together. She is an ideal friend.

I am proud of my best friend Neru. I hope we will be friends forever.

## MY DAILY ROUTINE

I have planned my schedule for the day. It has made me regular and punctual.

Daily I get up at 5.30 a.m I brush my teeth and answer nature's call. Then I go out for a morning walk. I come back at 6.30 o' clock and take my bath.

I pray to God and learn my lesson. Then I have my breakfast and leave for my school. I take my lunch during recess period.

I return home in the afternoon. I take rest for some time. Then I watch TV. programme and take tea.

Then I finish my home work. After that I go out and play for one hour.

In the evening, I help my mother in the kitchen. I take my supper and study for two hours.

Again I listen to TV. news. I drink a glass of milk.

I prepare my bag. Last of all I pray to God, wish my parents good night and go to bed at 9 o'clock.

## MY VILLAGE

My name is Mohit Verma. The name of my village is Jind. It is the biggest village in Haryana. There are about 1500 houses in my village.

Its population is about 45000. The chief occupation is agriculture. A pucca road passes through our village.

Morning and evening, people are always busy in fields, preparing the lands, manuring it, feeding the cattle and harvesting.

Some of them take weaving and spinning. Some are engaged in cottage industries.

Some of the houses are pucca but most of the houses are built of mud. There is an intermediate college and a Junior High School in the village.

There are five temples in it. There are two Bank in it. Middle class families lives here.

The villagers have love for education. But a very few boys read there. Instead of reading, they work in their fields. There is a small dispensary in our village. There is also a post office in my village.

My people lead a simple and happy life. They enjoy a good health. Real life is there in them. They are honest.

My village is making progress. I like it. I pray to God to give them moral courage so that they may lead a happy life.

## MY BIRTHDAY PARTY

A birthday party is an important function these days. It is an occasion for fun and enjoyment.

Relatives and friends are invited to take part in this function. They are served with sweets, fruits and tea or cold drinks.

My birthday falls on 20th May. This year I had a special programme for its celebration. I invited about 50 friends and relatives to participate in the function.

They brought for me beautiful and costly presents. The drawing room of our house was tastefully decorated.

Chairs and tables were laid for the guests. A big birthday cake was placed in the middle. I lighted the birthday candles. I cut the cake with a knife. All present wished me a happy birthday.

They followed the amusement programmes. Some of my friends sang sweet songs. Some showed mono-acting and dance. My relative garlanded me.

In the end we had a light refreshment. My parents blessed me and my relatives and friends wished me long life and prosperity.

## MY FAVOURITE GAME

Games are food for the body. They keep us fit and fresh. They teach us the value of discipline. Therefore, they are of great importance.

My most favourite game is Football. It is a world famous game.

Football is such a popular game that it is played even in the most remote corner of my country.

But it is a very hard game. It requires a lot of strength to kick the ball. They must also be skillful in controlling the ball.

All this makes the game a difficult game indeed. Playing football however help us healthy and active.

People walk long distances to watch a football match. Even old people enjoy watching this game.

To play this most interesting, I go to the field near my house where my friends wait for me every late afternoon.

My friends also love this game very much. We play until dark. I shall always love this game.

## MY FAVOURITE BOOK

The books are a true friends. They guide our life. They make us know the world around us.

I have read many books written by different authors, but the Ramayana is my favourite book. It is a holy book. It is a sacred book of the Hindus.

I feel happy on reading about the death of proudy Ravana and his relatives. We should follow the example of Lord Rama, Laskshman, Bharat and Hanuman.

A great-wise man wrote them. His name is Saint Tulsi Das. The Ramayana is one of the best book in the world. It guides me like a faithful teacher.

It has been translated into many languages. He provided a key to all problems in life. This book was given to me as a present by my aunt.

I like to read and re-read them. Many of them I remember very well. I like to tell them to my friends and my younger sister.

It makes me successful in every walk of life. I am lucky to have it. In short, it is a source of knowledge, wisdom and light.

## MY FAVOURITE FESTIVAL

There are many festivals which the Hindu celebrate in India. Diwali is one of them. Diwali is my favourite festival. It is a festival of lights, and joy.

Houses, shops and all other buildings are decorated with the lamps at night. Almost everyone in India celebrates this festival.

Diwali is one of the four greatest festivals of India. This festival marks the beginning of winter season. The people whitewash and paint their homes before

Deepawali. They wear new clothes and buy new utensils.

Children are thrilled with lights, crackers and sweets. The homes are lighted and decorated and people exchange sweets, and gifts.

At night people worship Laxmi, the goddess of wealth. Shop-keepers begin new account books on this day. On this day God Rama returned to Ayodhya after fourteen years of exile. The people of Ayodhya were very happy.

Diwali is indeed a beautiful festival which brings light and joy in all the homes and hearts. The Jains believe that Mahavir Swami had got Nirvana on this day.

## OUR SCHOOL LIBRARY

Our school library is housed in a big room. It is room of recreation and information. There is a big table in the centre.

There are more than five thousand books on almost all subjects in our library. The books are kept in the almirahs. The newspaper and many magazine stands are placed in a corner.

Sixty students can sit on benches.They read newspapers and magazines. There is a pin drop silence in the library.

There are five big almirahs. The almirahs are made of Iron and glass. Books are arranged on them.

The library is looked after by the librarian. He guides in selecting good books.

The students return the old books. They borrow fresh books. A student can borrow two books at a time.

I visit the library regularly. I like my school library very much.

## OUR SCHOOL ANNUAL DAY

Last Sunday was our school Annual Day. We had been preparing for it since a long time. We had arranged a military band to play the music for the March Past.

Parents were invited to the annual day and thus caused a great deal of excitement in our hearts. There were races organized. Every student hoped that he may be able to win the first prize at these events.

We had students dancing the Tamasha of Maharashtra, the Garbha of Gujarat, the Bhangara of Punjab and the western dance of Goa.

Another highlight of the Annual day was the flag hoisting

by the Chief Guest. After the speech of the Chief Guest, our principal also delivered his speech.

The Chief Guest gave away the prizes. I won the prize for coming first in the race.

The Principal then thanked the Chief Guest and other guests. We all await the arrival of our annual day every year. We love our school Annual Day.

## OUR NATIONAL LANGUAGE

India is a vast country. It is a land of divergent communities, divergent caste, divergent language, divergent manners and customs.

The multiplicity of language when the bus was advancing towards my destination, I started moving towards the exit door.

I could hardly set my foot on the ground, when the bus moved. I fell headlong on the road. To my surprise, some pick pocket had relieved me of my purse.

The button of my shirt was missing. I thanked God that I was alive.

It is generally understood that in India National Language changes after every 100 km.

## OUR SCHOOL PEON

A peon is an important person in all schools. Kishan Lal is our school peon. He is about thirty years old. He wears a khaki uniform and a cap on his head.

He is very useful for the school. His family lives in a village. He has various duties. He comes before the opening time of the school. He opens the doors and windows of the class rooms.

He cleans our classrooms. He puts things in order. When he is free, he sits on the bench outside the Principal's office. He has to work very hard.

He does not permit anybody to enter the school without the permission of the Principal. He carries out the Principal's orders. The Principal has full faith in him.

He helps everyone. He obeys the orders of the Principal and teachers. When it is time to go home, he rings the bell. All the students like him.

## BAISAKHI

The Baisakhi festival is celebrated all over Haryana

and Punjab. This seasonal festival falls on 13th of April.

The people put on new clothes and prepare special food items on this day. A fair is held in every town in connection with the Baisakhi festival. A temporary bazaar is set up.

Sweets, toys, fruits and other items of household needs are sold there. The merry-go-rounds attract ladies and children. The jugglers and acrobats show their feats. All class of the people visit the fair.

The farmers give a show of their country dance with the beating of the drum. There is great excitement and enthusiasm among the dancers.

The Baisakhi is the festival of their corn and crops. Even the elderly people and the ladies join the dancers forgetting their sense of shyness.

The saintly people sing hymns and deliver religious sermons. They do not care for worldy attachment.

## HOLI

India is a land of festivals. Holi is one of the most popular festivals one of them. It is observed on the full moon night of Phalguna. It marks the beginning of a new season.

Now the winter ends and spring begins. It is a two day festival. On the first night a bonefire is lighted. People gather around the fire and make merry.

The next day morning the festival of Holi starts. People throw coloured water, baloons and coloured powder on each other.

They beat drums and dance with joy. Their slogan is 'Holi Hai'. Some people celebrate it in a dirty way. It should be stopped by the police.

Holi reminds us of Bhakta Prahalad. Prahalad was a great devotee of God. But his father, a big demon, forbade him to remember God. The demon father tried to kill Prahalad by various means.

One day he put Prahalad into a blazing fire. But by the grace of God, Prahalad came out of the fire alive and unscathed.

## DUSSEHRA

Dusshera is a Hindu festival. It is celebrated on Danshvi (10th day) of lunar month. It is celebrated in the memory of Lord Rama.

He defeated Ravana, an evil soul on this day. Ravana was the king of Lanka. Bengalis believe that Durga came on the earth on this day.

The meaning of Durga is victory of good over evil. The effigies of the demon kings, Ravana, Kumbhkarna and Meghnath are burnt.

The play of Ramayana are staged and fairs are arranged all over the country. People feast and distribute sweets.

The children wear new clothes and get toys and sweet. Businessmen worship their account books on this day.

Dussehra not only brings joy but also inspires us to win over our bad instincts by good deeds and pious thoughts.

## CHRISTMAS

Christmas is an important Christian festival. It is celebrated all over the world. It falls on 25th December every year. December 25 is the birthday of Jesus Christ.

Fairs are held and shops set up on this occasion. Before it comes, people decorate their houses, shops, establishments, churches etc.

People in their best clothes attend the special services in Churches. They make christmas cakes. It is a festival of feasting, rejoicing and giving and receiving gifts.

The festivity begins on the Christmas Eve with carol singing and exchange of visits. It is a week long festival.

On the final day there is a mid-night mass, followed by ringing of the bells ushering in the New Year.

Christmas trees are erected and there is a lot of fun and merry-making. The members of a family living at different places join together to celebrate Christmas.

1st January is the New year Day. People exchange greetings and wish a happy New Year to one another. It is a public holiday and government offices etc. are closed.

## DIWALI

My favourite festival is Diwali. This is a festival of lights and sound. It is an important and popular Hindu festival. It is celebrated all over India and world.

Laxmi Pooja is performed on this day. Shop-keepers perform this Pooja in their shops as well as at home.

And new accounts are opened. People greet their relatives and friends with sweets and crackers.

The houses are completely cleaned and whitewashed. As the evening approaches the houses are lit with candles and electric lights.

At night crackers are fired. Children are warned to be

careful while bursting crackers because any neglect could cause burns.

Diwali marks the coming of the new season. It marks the return of Lord Rama to Ayodhya after his victory over Ravana.

Diwali brings peace and joy and this makes it my favourite festival.

# BHAI DOOJ

Bhai dooj festival is very popular and well known festival which can be celebrated across in India. This festival is celebrated after the two days of deepawali.

This festival is also known as Bhai-Tika and Bhatri-Ditya etc. It is festival of love and happiness between brother & sister. On this day married sister come their family and celebrate this festival with happiness.

Early morning sister wear new cloth and prepeir pooja for their brother and performed aarti of their brother on this day. All sister look like happy on this day. The brother give their sister sweets, chocolates and gifts on this day.

Women and girls make sweet dish and delicious food at home for their family and specially their brother. Then at evening time all of family members get together and take food.

## REPUBLIC DAY

On 26th January, 1950, our Constitution was introduced and our country became a Democratic Republic.

A speacial parade is organised in Delhi at Vijay Chowk. All the three armed forces of our country take part in the parade.

The President of India takes the salute of the Republic Day Parade.The country proudly displays her might through the guns tanks, ships and aeroplanes.

Folk dances and folk songs are performed by artists of different states.

Flower petals are showered from the air. Green, orange and white colour balloons float in the air. On this day every Indian feels proud to be the citizen of such a big democratic country.

## THE CHILDREN'S DAY

Every year, on 14th November, children celebrate our first Prime Minister Pandit Jawaharlal Nehru's birthday.

He was a great lover of children. Children called him 'Chacha' out of love and affection. This year also it was celebrated in our school with great pomp and show.

Principal gave a speech telling the students how they were dear to Chacha Nehru. School building was profusely decorated with small flags, buntings and balloons.

A cultural programme was organised. Dances, songs and one Act play was staged. Sports were held. The winners were given the prizes.

All the arrangements were made by the students. The children will never forget their Chacha Jawahar Lal Nehru.

## INDEPENDENCE DAY

15th August is our Independence Day. On this day we won our freedom from foreign rule. It is celebrated in every village, town and city of India.

But the main function is held at the Red Fort in Delhi where the Prime Minister hoists the National Flag.

He delivers a speech emphasizing the importance of national unity and integrity of India.

He reminds the people of the great sacrifices made by the Indian leaders to achieve independence. It is a day of national holiday.

Celebrations are also held in the state capitals. The Governor of some other State dignitary unfurls the national flag.

Our school also celebrates this occasion. It reminds us of the martyrs. It reminds us of the responsibility we owe to the nation.

## A VISIT TO A HILL STATION

Last year, the summer season was very hot. One day, I went to Mussoorie with my friends. It took seven hours from Delhi to Dehradun by train.

Then we hired a car and reached Mussoorie. Mussoorie is a beautiful hill station. The scenery on the way was very charming. First we went to see Kempty Falls. We spent the night in a hotel. All the hotels, coffee houses and restaurants were full of tourists.

Next day went to see the Gun Hill and Company Garden. We spent two hours in thc Company Garden. After lunch we roamed through the market. Lastly, we went to see Mussoorie Public School. Its compound is very beautiful.

We saw all the important places there. All of us were very happy. We decided to go back home. Soon we were travelling back and we reached home late at night. The memories of the visit still linger in my mind.

## A VISIT TO A HISTORICAL BUILDING (THE TAJ)

Last summer vacations I went to Agra to see the Taj Mahal with my family.

There are many historical buildings at Agra. But the most famous and the beautiful is the Taj Mahal.

The Taj Mahal stands on the bank of the river Jamuna. It took twenty thousand workmen and twenty-two years to build it.

The Taj Mahal was built by Shah Jahan in the memory of his wife Mumtaz Mahal.

Taj Mahal is built entirely of white marble. It is very grand historical building. In front of Taj there are beautiful fountains and parks.

People come from far and wide to see the Taj. I was very curious to know more about the Taj.

Taj Mahal is regarded as one of the seven wonders of the world. The Taj seems to glow in the light of the full moon. In a moon light night we stayed there for about two hours.

Then we came back. I cannot forget the night. It was my first visit to a historical building. It was a happy day for me.

## A VISIT TO MUSEUM

Our school organised on a picnic yesterday. We were taken to a Natural History Museum in Delhi.

A visit to a museum imparts us knowledge about the civilisation of the past. We saw swords, shields, daggers and other weapons of war.

We also saw the dresses used by the soldiers of the olden times. We saw ancient toys, utensils and other household goods.

We saw old coins of India. We also saw many statues, pictures and portraits there. The statues were of gods and goddesses. They were made of bronze, marble or copper.

There are records of the achievements made by Indian states after independence. I was very happy to see all these things.

## A VISIT TO THE RAILWAY STATION

I live in Delhi. It has a big railway station. I went to the station to receive my friend. He was coming from Punjab.

I bought a platform ticket and went in. My friend's train was late by forty minutes. So, I decided to take a look around.

There was a huge crowd on the platform. At the windows of the booking office there were long queues of people.

They were buying tickets for their journey. At enquiry window also there was big crowd. The hawkers were shouting at the top of their voice.

They were selling food, tea, newspaper etc. Soon, I saw the train coming. My friend came out and he was very happy to see me. We came home in an autorickshaw.

## A VISIT TO THE CIRCUS

I like the circus show very much. Last Month the Gemini Circus came to our town. It brings actors, acrobats and performers from various parts of the country. They perform tricks that attract everybody and people like to visit the circus again and again.

We reached the circus gate at 4.00 pm and purchased our tickets for the entrance. We sat down comfortably with our packets of chips and popcorn, when all of a sudden we heard the loud trumpeting of an elephant.

An acrobat sat on the elephant's back. She suddenly began to perform on his back, she would turn around and sometimes stand on her head or on one hand. The horse was trotting around on the ring.

The jokers cheered us all up a lot. They were dressed in colourful clothes and their faces were painted with beautiful colours which made them look very funny.

The gymnasts performed for an hour. The bodies of these gymnasts are very supple and it is amazing to see them moving their body as through it were rubber.

## A VISIT TO FAIR

The fairs are common in our life. They make our life enjoyable. People wait eagerly for them as they enjoy themselves on these days.

Almost all fairs are common in villages, towns and cities. But in cities the fairs are much bigger and are held with more pomp and show.

In Delhi, Diwali fairs have become very famous. At every festival, a number of fairs are held in different corners of the city.

This year, I went to see a grand fair held at Ramlila Grounds during Diwali. I went with my parents. We went there by bus.

The bus was packed with people and roads were unusually busy. People were going to different directions.

At Ramlila grounds, there was a huge crowd of people at the entry itself. One had to get in a queue for the entry tickets. After getting tickets we entered the fair.

It was all very colourful. Two elephants were there at the entrance to welcome the people.

In the fair, there were over 200 stalls of different items. The sweet stalls were over-crowded. People were standing in queue for their turn to come.

The sweet sellers were doing brisk business. My mother wanted to do some shopping, so we went to different stalls which had clothes, utensils, handicraft and jewellery.

There was one stall I liked very much. It was full of wooden toys. My father bought me a wooden doll and a soldier.

They were really beautiful and looked real. Children were buying toys, fireworks and candles. I also bought some candles and fire works.

Some children were taking free rides on horses and camels. I also enjoyed a ride on the horse. After roaming about, we felt hungry. We had food at food stall. It was neat and clean. After food, I also had a cold drink.

While coming back, I pleaded with my father to take a ride on the merry-go-round. All of us enjoyed the ride very much. It was a good fun.

After the ride, we started for home. It was a day which I thoroughly enjoyed. Fairs are a lot of fun.

## A VISIT TO A HOSPITAL

A hospital is an institution in which sick and injured persons are given medical or surgical treatment.

Last week I happened to visit the local hospital. There was a great rush of visitors in the compound who came to meet their patients.

My uncle had been admitted there for an operation of his heart. There were many other patients. They were suffering from different diseases.

A young woman was lying with serious burns. In the next ward a man had been stabbed in the back. Doctors and nurses were moving about.

They were attending to the patients. They were full of love and sympathy. The hospital presented a horrible look.

I felt very sad and returned home in a contemplative mood.

## A VISIT TO EXHIBITION

Last Sunday, I visited an art exhibition held in the capital. It was arranged in the famous Sahitya Kala Akademi. I went there with my friends. I am very fond of paintings.

The exhibition had the paintings of many famous artists like M.F. Hussain, Manjit Bawa and Sanyal. There were many visitors to this exhibition as all these artists are very well known all over the world.

Their works were on sale. The painting were costly. So, I could not buy any painting. I enjoyed seeing such fine pieces of art.

I met students from the art school and made friends with them. I want to be a painter when I grow up.

This exhibition gave me a lot of inspiration and encouragement.

## A VISIT TO A ZOO

One Sunday, I went to see the Delhi Zoo with my family. We bought the tickets and entered the gate. The animals were leading a natural life there.

There were many birds and animals. My brother and I were surprised to see so many birds and animals. The birds were chirping in different notes and making a lot of noise.

The ducks, swans and some other birds were swimming in the pond. Some animals were kept in cages. We saw a white peacock there.

Fierce animals like tigers, lions, leopards, were roaring in their cages. There was a white tiger too. What a beautiful tiger that was!

The zoo is very big. We felt tired and sat down under a tree and ate food. At 5 P.M. we again started our round of the zoo.

The deer and monkeys were playing. An elephant was eating sugarcane. There was a chimpanzee sitting in a cage. We shook hands with him.

I gathered much knowledge about the animals. In the evening we came back home. The visit to the zoo will always be remembered by me.

# A CHAIR

I love my own chair to sit in. It is very beautiful. Some chairs are made of cane and iron. But it is made of wood. It is very comfortable. It is well polished and shining.

My father bought it from a furniture shop. He gave it to me as a birthday gift. Its price is Rs. 450. It is dark brown in colour. The carpenter made it.

There are many kinds of chairs. Such chairs are very costly. Lawyers, Doctors or Officers use them.

I always sit in my chair for study. It is in my study room. It has four legs, one seat and two arms. It has a long back also.

It is very comfortable to sit on. I sit on this chair to do my school home work. It is very useful to me. I like it very much.

# A COLD DAY

It was the month of December last year. It was the coldest day of the winter season. People were finding it difficult to walk on the road. Woolen clothes were of no help.

In the morning my mother brought two hot 'potato's pranthas' with hot milk for me. I took my breakfast and left for school.

There I found every child shivering with cold even when he was covered in sweaters and a thick coat. In school our teachers taught us with all the doors and windows shut.

During the recess period there was a great rush in the canteen. The students took tea in large amounts.

As I returned from school, I passed through the local market. Very few customers had come to make purchases.

From the evening cool wind started blowing. The sky started getting over-casted. Every one was seen in his warm clothes. Vehicles were driven with their lights on. Nothing was visible clearly.

Sunlight looked like a moonlight. Fog was seen everywhere. I was in my house. I was shivering with cold. We all sat by the fire. My mother gave us hot coffee.

We kept the doors closed all the day long. Whenever I remember it, my body begins to shiver. In fact I cannot forget this cold day.

## A HOT DAY IN SUMMER

In India, it is very hot in the months of May and June. During these moths people remain indoors and they avoid going out. 24th June was the hottest day of the year. It is very hot day.

There was no movement in the air. The sky was clear. Everyone perspired from top to toe.

Most of the people shut themselves up in the their houses. They felt thirsty again and again. The rich took shelter under the airconditioners.

The poor used hand fans. But no one felt comfortable. There was no traffic on the roads.

Seven cases of heat stroke were reported on that day. There was a general cry for rain. Everyone seemed to be tired of life.

## A RAINY DAY IN SUMMER

A Rainy day in summer makes the weather pleasant. One day, it was hot. There was no movement in the air.

People were sweating, and to protect themselves from hot air they took shelter in their rooms under airconditioners and coolers.

All of a sudden, clouds appeared. Soon, the whole sky was overcast. It became dark. Lightning began to thunder. It began ro rain.

Children ran out in the streets and enjoyed the rain very much. It rained continuously for two hours. After the rain stopped, ground became slippery.

Some of the people actually slipped. It made the bystanders laugh. In spite of all inconvenience, the people heaved a sigh of relief.

## A MARKET SCENE

There are many markets in Delhi. Chandni Chowk, Tilak Nagar, Lajpat Nagar, Sarojini Nagar and

Connaught Place are some of the big and famous markets.

I live in Karol Bagh. It has big market. The market of the colony is a very busy place. There are a large number of show rooms and shops.

I went to the market with my mother yesterday. We bought my school shoes and dress.

My mother also bought some bangles. There was a lot of noise in the market. People from all walks of life are seen shopping around.

Some shopkeepers do roaring business. Police keep watch on bad elements. I had a fruit chat. I love to go to the market.

## A HOUSE ON FIRE

In the evening of last Sunday I found that the house of our neighbour had caught fire. The flames were rising to the sky.

Suddenly I heard shouts of "Fire, Fire!" I woke up at once and looked out in the street. I saw a house on fire.

I ran downstairs and reached the place. Many people had collected there. They were running with buckets full of water and bags full of sand. What a terrible scene I saw that day!

But it did not prove of much help. A strong wind was blowing. Some cries were heard from inside the house. The house belonged to a doctor.

Soon some fire-engines reached the spot. Two firemen entered the burning house. They helped the doctor's family to come out. Fortunately no one was killed.

The fire was brought under control. The building was reduced to ashes. The shopkeeper had suffered a great loss. It was a very fearful sight.

## A MORNING WALK

There is nothing like a morning Walk to give a good start to our day. It makes early rising a regular habit. It showers untold blessings upon its undertakers.

Nature shows herself at her best around the morning Everything is calm and quiet all around. The plants in parks and gardens and the dew drops sparkling on the green grass soothe the eyes and the hearts.

The trees provide us with oxygen. It gives energy to our lungs. The morning breeze is unpolluted. Nature looks fresh and fills our hearts with happiness.

A morning walk is the best tonic for the aged and ailing person. It is a permanent cure for many ailments. Brisk walking is a useful and healthful exercise.

## A VILLAGE FAIR

I decided to see the village fair with my parents. We reached the fair at 12 A.M. It was held at a two miles away from Delhi.

A number of people had come to see the fair. There are many shops in the fair. Some sold ice-creams and some sold fruits chat.

There was a rush of children on the shop of toys and dolls. Many children were enjoyed elephant-ride. Bangel-sellers' were having brisk business.

A magician was showing his magic. It attracted a large crowd. My father bought some toys for us and my mother bought some bangles. We enjoyed the fair very much.

## AN IDEAL CITIZEN

An ideal citizen is one, who gives utmost importance to his country and countrymen. He thinks about them first, and then about himself. He thinks more about his duties than his rights.

An ideal citizen always thinks about the progress of his country. He has full political awareness. He knows what is good for his country and what is bad. He observes all his duties devotedly.

He never forgets to caste his vote. He considers the qualities of her candidate before casting his vote. No greet can compel him to take a wrong decision.

An ideal citizen is above caste, creed, religion and region. He works to help the poor and the downtrodden. He is social and shares others problem.

He never considers his personal interests superior to others. He always tries to protect national properties.

He is law-abiding. He pays his taxes honestly. He never encourages nepotism, corruption, dishonesty, favourism etc. He never pays or takes bribe. He believes in law and order of the country.

He is aware of national and international affairs. So he does everything, he can do for his country.

## AN IDEAL STUDENT

An ideal student is one who is all around the best student. Kamal is an ideal student in my class.

He believes in simple living and high thinking. He helps the needy and sympathies with the poor.

He does not mix up with the bad boys. He never tells a lie. He always speaks the truth.

He is not a book worm. He is a good player also. He never quarrels with anybody.

He is a very well behaved boy. He loves everybody and everybody loves him.

Most of the people now think that we are real brother. I like him the most. I am really proud of my friend.

## AN INDIAN FARMER

An Indian farmer is the backbone of the society. He grows corn, vegetables and fruits for our food and cotton for our clothes. He is a hard working man.

He works from morning till evening in the scorching heat and biting cold. Early in the morning he drives his oxen to the fields. He ploughs the fields, sows seeds and waters the plants.

He looks after the crops and saves them from being spoiled by stray cattle or wild animals. He enjoys no holiday.

At noon he takes his meals under a shady tree and then takes a little rest. In the evening he returns home, tired and exhausted.

But he leads a simple life. He lives in a mud house, eats simple food and wears coarse clothes. Generally he is illiterate.

When the crop ripens, he feels happy. He reaps it, thrashes it and takes the corn to the market. In times of a bad harvest he has little money to buy seeds and manure and runs into debt.

He believes in old customs and superstitions. His cattle are his most valuable property. Often during drought crops fail and he is in trouble.

The farmer is fond of festivities. He spends lavishly on marriages and other social ceremonies.

Recently, the use of agricultural machinery and chemical manures and the provision of credit facilities by cooperative societies and rural banks has improved his lot and changed his outlook on life.

## AN ACCIDENT I SAW

It was a cold day. There was some fog and not much traffic on the road. I was standing in the balcony of my house. Suddenly I heard a loud noise.

The driver of a car lost his balance at a turn. He crashed into an electric pole. I rushed for rescue. Many other people also came running.

The driver was badly hurt. We helped him to come out of the car. He had received a big cut on the forehead. He was profusely bleeding. Soon he was carried away in a car to the hospital.

The driver was the only person in the car. The car was badly smashed. A pool of blood had collected on the road.

After sometime a team of traffic police came. They cleared away the crowd. Then they began their investigation.

It was a horrible experience. I could not believe my eyes. It all happened in no time. I still feel frightened when I remember the accident.

# AN EVENING WALK

The daily walks was excellent exercises. They refresh our mind as well as soul. A morning walk and an evening walk have their own charms and importance.

I go for a walk around 7 o'clock in the evening. My mother accompanies me. Both of us enjoy this walk.

In the evening the streets and roads are quite congested due to the rush of traffic. So we go to a park which is nearby to our house.

There I meet my friends and play with them. The people of all ages come in the evening for walks. The old men form a group and discuss their matters.

After we finish playing with our friends, we sit on the grass and relax. It is a very beautiful sight. The birds are also flying back to their nests in a group.

A evening walk is the best tonic for the aged and ailing person. It is a permanent cure for many ailments. This is the walk which I enjoy the most.

# THE DOG

The dog is a pet animal. A dog is a faithful friend. It is very useful. A street dog is a common thing.

Dogs are of many kinds. They are of different colours. Usually they are of brown, black, white and red colours.

A dog is kept as a pet to protect a house and family. A dog barks whenever it sees a stranger or a thief. Its loud bark makes the people alert and watchful. It is very faithful and obedient animal.

A dog has four legs, two ears and a long tail. It lives on milk, bread and meat. All dogs have very bright and intelligent eyes. It has a very strong sense of smell. The Police keep and train it to catch thieves.

A mad dog is a dangerous animal. The bite of a mad dog may prove fatal. We should take care that our pet dogs do not become mad. We should also see that they are not bitten by a mad dog.

A dog is also used for hunting. Children love to play with dogs. A young one of a dog is called a puppy. A female dog is called a bitch.

# THE HORSE

A horse is an useful animal. It is a great friend of man. It is clever and can learn many tricks. It serves its master faithfully. It can dance and jump.

The horse has big eyes. It uses its long tail for flicking away flies. It has long, strong legs. It can run long distances.

Some horses can run fast. Some can pull heavy loads. In olden days, horses were used to carry people and goods from place to place.

The horse is a great friend of man. Man's love for the horse is well-known. The Arabian horses are famous. The horses live mainly on grass. It also likes grams.

An adult male horse is called 'stallion', the female, 'mare'. A male baby horse is called a colt. A female baby horse is called a foal.

Today, people use horses for riding, racing, pulling carts, and in the circus.

# THE ELEPHANT

An elephant is a very large and wise animal. It is huge and has four feet. It has legs which look like pillars. Its skin colour is dark grey. White elephants are also there. But they are rare.

It has two large fan-like ears. It has a short tail. It has a long and powerful trunk. It is so wonderful that it can pick up even a pin. With its trunk an elephant sucks water and eats its food.

A male elephant has long curved tusks. The tusks are very costly. They are used as ivory for making beautiful things.

It is a very useful animal. It helps us carry large wood logs from the jungle. It is used for hunting and riding.

It has a very sharp memory. It never forgets a kindness or unkindness shown to it. Its keeper is called a 'mahout'. When it walks it looks quite royal.

After the death of an elephant, its teeth are used for making ornaments, decoration pieces, and for many other purposes.

Elephants can be seen in a circus doing many tricks. They can also be seen in marriages and religious processions. An elephant trumpets.

# THE COW

The cow has been one of the important domestic animals. She gives us milk, and her calf, when grown up to an ox, helps in our agricultural work. Cow-dung is used as manure and fuel.

It's milk are very useful for us. We obtain butter, ghee, curds, cheese, etc. from milk. A cow is regarded as 'mother' and worshipped by the Hindus.

The cow has a strong and heavy body with four legs. Her body is covered with short hair. She has a pair of horns and a long tail.

Her eyes are big and beautiful. The feet are hoofed and the hoofs are split in the middle.

Cow-milk is very nutritious and easily digestible. This milk can be consumed in many forms. It is also available in powder form and condensed.

Cows have different colours. They are found everywhere in the world. Cow is a holy animal for Hindus.

Cow is very useful for us in many ways. So we should treat them kindly and look after them.

# THE CROW

This is a crow. It is an ugly bird. It is seen every where. The crow is black in colour. Its chest is of ash colour.

It has two little disshaped legs. It is a big bird. Its neck is grey. It has sharp eyesight.

The crow is greedy bird. Its eye-sight is defective. The crow is the most cunning bird in the world. It has a harsh voice. Its beak is strong and big. It caws loudly.

Crows live on trees and in big groups. Crow is a very common bird. It picks up worms, small fish and frogs with its short beak.

It also eats crumbs of bread and other things. It is afraid of men and animals, especially dogs. It snatches breads from small children.

The call of a crow is not pleasing because it is harsh. It is a very clever and cunning bird. I do not hate it.

## THE CAMEL

The camel is a large animal. It has very tall legs and a long neck. It has a high hump. It does not look so beautiful.

It can walk and run easily in desert. This is why the camel is called the ship of the desert.

It has a very big bag in his stomach. It stores water and food in the hump. So it can stay without water and food for many days. Its feet are padded. These pads help him in walking or running on the sand.

A camel can tell of coming sand-storm. It can warn man of a possible storm. The camels from Arabia have one hump. The Bactarian camels have two humps.

A camel is a very useful animal. It carries load and draws carts. It is used for ploughing the field and drawing water.

## THE PERSON I LIKE MOST

Pandit Jawahar Lal Nehru is the person I like most. He has impressed me greatly. He was born on 14th

November, 1889 in Allahabad. Moti Lal Nehru was his father. He was a great lawyer.

Jawaharlal Nehru got his early education at home. The he went to England for higher studies. He returned to India in 1912. Later he became a lawyer.

He gave up his practice and joined the freedom movement under Mahatma Gandhi. He was totally involved in India's freedom movement.

He was sent to jail several times. In 1947 when India became free, he was elected the first Prime Minister.

He was a great statesman, idealist and a dreamer. He has written many books. He worked hard to serve his country.

Pandit Nehru loved children. And the children called him Chacha Nehru with love. He always liked and enjoyed the company of children.

He always wore a rose in his dress. His birthday is now celebrated as Children's Day.

India made great progress under his leadership. He died on 27th May, 1964. He was one of the builders of modern India. We always remember him fondly.

## THE TEACHER I LIKE MOST

All the teachers in our school are good, able and well-qualified. All of us respect them and obey them. They also love us.

But my favourite teachers is Mr. Veer Singh He has great impression on my personality. He is our class-incharge.

Mr. Singh is well built, tall and a strong man. He always dress-up smartly. He is always neat and clean. He has a pleasing personality. He is a well-mannered person.

He always smiles and never looses his temper. He is respected by all of us. He is polite and soft spoken. He is always regular and punctual.

He teaches us English and is the master of the subject. He makes every student understand his lesson well. One can never forget, whatever he teaches. He has made English grammar very easy for us.

He keeps strict discipline in the class. He never beats anyone, still boys always follow his orders. He never allows anybody to take liberty with him.

He is a good sportsman. He is a very good cricket player. He encourages students to take part in games.

He is respected by all teachers, students and other staff of the School. Principal considers him, his right hand and has full faith in him. He will always remain a source of inspiration for me.

## THE STREET HAWKER

We find street hawkers in all big cities. They are poor people, so they are not in a position to run a rented shop. They sell their things from street to street. They make our lives easier also.

Hawkers are found selling vegetables and fruits since morning. Some hawkers have big baskets on their heads full of fruits or vegetables while others have bicycles which make their job easier.

They sell fresh vegetables. Old and busy people, who cannot manage to go to markets, welcome the hawkers. The housewives wait for them eagerly.

Kamal Kant is our street hawker. He comes early in the morning at 8 a.m. My mother waits for his arrival. He shouts at the top of his voice to announce his arrival. There are all vegetables of the season. He is young/and sturdy.

He charges less money than the shops in the markets. He is a clever salesman. He believes in less profit but more sale.

He has some permanent customers in our locality. He has studied upto 6th standard. He knows some English.

He shouts very loudly. He is good at arithematics. He calculates money in no time. He is an awakened citizen.

He discusses some politics sometimes. He has a small family of two children only. He has a desire to educate them.

During the whole day, we find a number of hawkers selling other goods in our streets. Children wait anxiously for the arrival of ice cream seller, while ladies and gents wait for 'Allu-Ki-Tikki Wala', 'Golgape Wala'.

Some lady hawkers sell utensils in exchange of old clothes. Sometimes we find these hawkers sell inferior things at cheap rate.

The middle class people prefer to buy goods from these hawkers and fulfil their needs with less money.

A street hawker leads a very hard life. He has to get up early in the morning and shout all the day.

Sometimes he befools the customers. He has a little sense of cleanliness.

He does not earn much. Usually, he lives in a small hut with his family and can hardly make both ends meet.

## THE POLICEMAN

A police man is a familiar figure. He wears a khaki uniform and belt on which his number is shown. He is a useful servant. He is tall and strong.

He is always alert. He puts on a batch on which his name is written. He performs his duty actively and regularly.

He catches thieves, robbers and bad characters at the risk of his life. He also arrests the smugglers, murderers and dacoits.

The policeman maintains law and order in his area. He guards our life and property. He patrols the streets during dark and chilly nights.

Traffic police controls traffic. He clears the traffic jams from the roads. He carries the injured people to the hospital.

The policeman's duty is hard and risky. Most of the policemen are dutiful and honest.

He is a faithful public-servant. He is our social protector. He is full of discipline. The duty of a policeman is very tough. We must respect a policeman.

# THE PRIZE DISTRIBUTION FUNCTION

The prize distribution function of our school was held in month of September, 2007. It was held in the school playground.

The school was cleaned and decorated. Many preparations were made. The guardians of the students were invited. The prizes were placed on the table.

The Education Minister of our pradesh was invited as a Chief Guest of the function. The Chief Guest arrived at 5 P.M.

He was warmly welcomed by the Principal and other staff members at the gate. The school band played a welcome tune.

Soon the programme started. The principal welcomed the chief guest. He thanked him for coming to the function. He request him to say a few words. The chief guest gave a short speech.

After this, the prize were given away by the chief guest. Many students got prizes. I was also one of the prize winners. All of us were very happy.

There are many interesting items. Many photographs were taken. The principal thanked the chief guest. The programme began with our national song.

The next day was announced a holiday. The function came to an end. We enjoyed the function very much.

## THE PEN FRIEND

Although I have many friends in India I have always wished for a friend who lives in a foreign country.

The other day I was reading the magazine "X-act Times" and I came across the addresses of various children all over the world who want to make pen friends.

I wanted a pen friend in the United States of America as I found the culture of that country very different from ours. Finally I found the address of Mary who lives in San Francisco.

She is fourteen years old. She wrote to me as soon as she received my first letter and I was very touched by her warmth and friend lines.

She is extremely lovely to. As she is the only child she writes to me about all her problems and I do the same.

We give each other a lot of support although we live so far from each other.

Pen friends are a lot of fun apart from being our confidants. They help to educate us and we find ourselves growing into persons whose horizons are as large as the world itself.

## THE STREET BEGGAR

Beggars are very common. They can be seen everywhere. They are found in the bus stops, market places, historical places, railway platforms, road sides and in parks.

Begging is really a curse. Begging has become a profession. Some beggars are healthy and do not deserve our sympathy.

But some beggars are lame, cripple or blind. They deserve our sympathy. Some beggars sing songs and play on musical instruments.

A beggar is a poor man. He goes about begging for food, clothes and money. There are many beggars who are disabled and handicapped.

We should take pity on them. They really deserve our help and charity. We should help a beggar if he is blind, lame or handicapped.

Many street beggars are thieves too. Therefore, they do not want to change their profession. They are lazy people. They do not want to work. We should be aware of such type of beggars.

We should help only those beggars who are disabled and cannot earn their livelihood by doing any kind of work.

Beggars are a nuisance. They are clever and cheat the public. Sometimes they steal, make places dirty and trouble the people by persistent begging. They should be discouraged. They spoil the image of our country.

## THE POSTMAN

All of us know the postman very well. He is an important public servant. He is of great service to us. He wears a khaki uniform.

He delivers letters, parcels, money orders and other things. These are from our relatives and friends. We cannot think of our life without a postman.

He has to go daily to many places to deliver letters, parcels, telegrams etc. He is welcome at every door. He does not enjoy many holidays. His salary is not high.

A postman is a hard-working person. Sometimes it is very cold, or very hot, or there is heavy rain, but he delivers letters without fail.

We wait for the postman eagerly every day. He brings letters from our friends and relations. I specially wait for him on my birthday and festivals. Then he brings many greeting cards and letters of good wishes.

A postman has to cover a particular area. Either he walks or rides a bicycle. He can be seen moving from place to place and house to house. In rural area he has to cover long distances.

We must respect him because he is very useful to us. He is just like our friend. He deserves our cooperation.

## THE RADIO

Radio is one of the most wonderful gift of science. Radio sets are very popular. They can be found in every home. It has made us feel the world small.

It helps us in sending news and message without wires. We can enjoy news, music, songs etc. from different part of the world through it sitting in our houses.

We also get lessons on radio at school. The programmes are broadcast all the twenty four hours from radio. Film songs and children programmes are of much interest.

Radio is also a powerful means of teaching. In short the radio is of great use and interest to all of us. Now we have pocket radios which are very convenient to carry.

# THE TELEVISION

The television is a great gift of modern science. It was invented by a scientist, Baird. These days it is very popular. It is a good source of entertainment.

Televisions have almost replaced the radios and transistors. There are many different programmes everyday on television.

There are films, songs, music, dramas, plays etc. to keep the viewers entertained.

Republic Day and Independence Day functions at national and regional levels are also shown on television.

Now people have colour televisions. It makes viewing more interesting and exciting.

The television is an improvement on the radio. With it we can see cultural programmes. It is also a great source of distance teaching and education. There are special school and college transmissions.

Thousands of students who cannot attend a school, college or a university are taught through it. Its appeal both to the eyes and the ears is great. It makes learning easy.

Though television is a very useful thing but, if we see it continuously it can effect our eye-sight.

## THE COLDEST DAY IN WINTER

In India, the winter season lasts from November to February. During these months it is very cold. The thirteenth of January was the coldest day.

The temperature had fallen below freezing point. Nothing was visible outside due to thick fog.

Everywhere only white fog was seen. Biting wind was blowing. Our teeth were chattering. We put the room-heater on.

All the members of our family sat around it in quilts or blankets. Mother served tea. The sun was nowhere to be seen.

I did not like missing the school. But I reached the school late. We did not move out during the recess.

As the last bell rang, we ran for our houses. Study is more convenient in winter. But that day was so cold that I could not study.

## WHY I LOVE BOOKS

I have a little library of my own at home. Now I have fairy tales, fun books, books on geography, science, history and literature - all of which are presented in the form of a story.

I love my books. Whenever I have a holiday, I pick up any book from the shelf and read it.

I get so engrossed in the book that I often forget to eat. My mother has to yell at me to have my lunch.

I often borrow books from my friends and my school library. Books hold a great charm for me. Some of my friends too have started enjoying reading books as much as I do.

Most of my relatives and friends know that the best birthday gift that they can give me is books and with their generosity I have over a hundred books in my personal library now.

## TO FEEL THE FRIENDSHIP

Friendship is a special boon of God given to man. You can share all types of sorrows and joys with a friend.

Good friends always give one the right kind of guidance. They are sincere and they make incredible sacrifices without any personal motive.

Good friends always stand by their friends in fair and foul weather. It may be easy to make a friend but "being a friend takes a life time". Friendship or being a friend is not a temporary phase.

It lasts for years and never breaks unless one of the two proves insincere. It is in fact a very delicate and sensitive relationship. It needs to be tackled carefully without hurting each other.

It is true that we can't make friends who are not similar to us in some way or the other. Two persons become friends when they have common ideas, tastes, approach to things and common value systems.

It is the real and clear understanding of each other that sustains friendship. Vices like arrogance, in flatedegos and vanity can be harmful to a friendship.

If one person tries to show his superiority over the other such a relation cannot last.

They should share each other's problems and joys and should be willing to help in the time of read.

Good friends can help to mould one's character hence we should always be careful of the kind of people we befriend and once we have a friend we should thank God for sending him to us.

# WONDERS OF SCIENCE

This is an age of science. Science has completely changed the entire world. Science has made our life more comfortable and trouble free.

Science is useful to us. The blessings of Science are too many to count. Science has conquered time and distance. Electricity is another wonderful gift of science.

Electricity, one of its off shoots, is used in washing clothes, cooking food and in entertaining us. Its uses are unlimited.

It lights our houses, shops, showrooms and streets. It runs our air-conditioners and air coolers. It keeps us warm in winter and cool in summer.

Mobile, television, radio, aeroplane etc. are some of these. It has increased our speed of work and has given us fast moving means of transport.

Travelling is now so safe and fast. We have cars, buses, metro-rails, trains, ships and aeroplanes. Man can walk and talk any corner of the world.

In the fields of education, entertainment and agriculture has proved a great blessing. The worst fact of science is seen in the wars.

Science is a boon and is in the service of man if used in the right manner.

## HUMAN BODY

Human body is wonderful thing. It is said that God created man in his own image.

The human skeleton is like a cage. It provides necessary support to our body. It also protects our various vital organs.

There are more than 200 bones in an adult person. These bones are made up of calcium and phosphorus. The box like skull protects the brain.

The muscles constitute the flesh. They are about 500 in number. Human body is made up of cells. A cell is a basic unit of the body. There are millions and millions of cells in a human body.

It is the cell which gets nourishment through food and drink and oxygen through breathing.

Then there are circulatory, respiratory, digestive and nervous systems. They all are wonderful in their own way. And human brain is the most wonderful creation.

The harmonious working of these different systems and organs give us good health. Really human body is a great marvel.

# NATIONAL ANIMAL OF INDIA-THE TIGER.

The magnificent Tiger Panthera tigris (linnaeus), the national animal of India, is a rich-colored well-striped animal with a short coat.

The combination of grace, strength, power has earned the tiger great respect and high esteem.

Indian tigers are famous all over the world and one of the main attractions for the lovers of wild life. They are the crowning glory and the light of the Indian wild life.

Tough, muscular, majestic tigers roam about the Sunderbans of Bengal "burning bright in the darkness of the night."

The natives of the forest worship the tiger as the deity that gives them honey and wax. The Sunderbans are their main habitat for their thick forests of Sunder trees.

They feed on fish, cattle and sometimes human beings. The man-eaters are the most dreaded of all wild beasts.

It is a common belief that a tiger does not harm anyone who has offered prayers to him. Tigers are fast runners, excellent swimmers and their eyesight is strong.

To check the dwindling population of tigers in India, which came down to just 1,827 in 1972, massive conservation program was initiated in April 1973, known as the 'Project Tiger'.

This project aims to maintain a viable population of tigers in India for scientific, economic, aesthetic, cultural and ecological values.

Since then, the tiger population has shown a gradual increase and the census of 1989 puts the tiger population of the country at 4,334.

So far, 19 tiger reserves have been established in the country under this project, covering over 29, 716 sq. km. forest area.

## NATIONAL BIRD OF INDIA-THE PEACOCK

Peacock is a large and majestic bird. It has got a long and beautiful tail. Both the peacock and the hen have crest. But the crest of hen is smaller in size.

The main body of the cock is mottled brown in color. Especially, the metallic green color found on the lower neck is very attractive. Though peacocks are beautiful looking birds their calls are loud and coarse.

They move in-groups and they are normally spotted in the forests, villages and nearby fields. They are shy in nature.

It feeds on lizards, snakes, grains and insects. The hen lays a maximum of five eggs, which are in pale cream color.

The significance of peacock is attached to cultures of India, Far East, Ancient Persia, Greek and Christian.

In Hinduism, the image of the god of thunder, rains and war, Indra, was depicted in the form of a peacock.

In south India, peacock is considered as a 'vahana' or vehilce of lord Muruga. The figure of peacock is painted in various Islamic religious buildings. In Christianity, the peacock was also known as the symbol of the 'Resurrection'.

In India people believe that whenever the cock spread its tails in an ornamental fashion, it indicates that rain is imminent. In a way it is partly true.

At the sight of dark clouds the bird outspreads its tail and starts dancing in rhythmic fashion.

Most of the folklore including Bharatha Natyam has got special dancing poses for the peacock dance.

## NATIONAL FLAG OF INDIA

National flag is the symbol of a country's freedom and sovereignty. It is the flag under which our freedom fighters had fought for India's Independence.

Before Independence, the National Flag had the spinning wheel placed at its centre. It was necessary at that time to do so to remind the people of the Swadeshi Movement started by Gandhiji along with the movement for freedom.

After Independence, the spinning wheel was replaced by the Ashok Chakra. The Ashok Chakra has 24 spokes. It stands for peace and love which enshrined the state of the famous emperor, Ashoka.

Our National flag is rectangular in shape. It has three horizontal bands. Each band is of a different colour. That is why the flag is also called the Tricolour or the Tiranga.

At the top is the saffron band which symbolises the spirit of sacrifice. The middle band is the white band which characterizes peace and truth.

It is in this band that the peace-spreading Ashoka Chakra is located, thus enhancing the significance of peace and love. At the bottom is the dark green band which stands for growth and prosperity.

The National flag is hoisted on important buildings of national importance on the occasion of national festivals. Now, the Supreme Court has given enough liberty to the people to fly the National flag.

But, all rules according to the relevant Act governing its hoisting, have to be followed. On the death of some celebrity, it flies half-mast over buildings.

It is imperative for us to respect our national flag and never let it down. We should be ready to lay down our life for its high position that it deserves.

## SCENE AT A BUS-STOP

Last Sunday we decided to visit the Trade Fair. We found a long queue at bus stop. Men and women, young and old, all were standing in a queue.

Some were talking about the politics. Some of them were gossiping. Some gentlemen were busy reading the newspapers.

All of them were waiting for the bus. In a few minutes the queue became longer than before.

After waiting for some times, we saw a bus coming. Every one became ready to board the bus. It did not stop at the stand and passed by us.

After sometime, we again saw a bus. It stopped. The queue broke. Young men can push, pull and drag others. But women simply cannot do this. Some young men boarded it. They remained helpless spectors.

The scene on a bus-stop shows how backward we Indians are. I have seen persons pushing down ladies, young and old, in their attempt to get into a bus.

We cancelled our programme. We decided to visit the Trade Fair some other day.

## DELHI METRO TRAIN

The Delhi Metro was started on 24th December 2002.

It has became the second underground rapid transit system in India, after Kolkata but Delhi Metro has a combination of elevated, at-grade and underground lines.

It has won numerous environmentally friendly awards from many reputed organisations including the United Nations, RINA, and ISO.

It was the first metro rail in the world to be ISO 14001 certified for its environmentally friendly construction.

Delhi Metro is a pride of Delhi. Now other states government are seeking Delhi Metro help to increase its lines to other states cities.

## TAJ MAHAL

Taj Mahal of India - "the epitome of love", "a monument of immeasurable beauty". The beauty of this magnificent monument is such that it is beyond the scope of words.

The thoughts that come into the mind while watching the Taj Mahal of Agra is not just its phenomenal beauty, but the immense love which was the reason behind its construction.

Mughal Emperor Shah Jahan got this monument constructed in the memory of his beloved wife Mumtaz Mahal, with whom he fell in love at the first sight. Ironically, the very first sight of the Taj Mahal, the epitome of love and romance, also leaves visitors mesmerized and perpetually enthralled.

Standing majestically on the banks of River Yamuna, the Taj Mahal is synonymous to love and romance. It is believed that the name "Taj Mahal" was derived from the name of Shah Jahan's wife, Mumtaz Mahal and means "Crown Palace".

The purity of the white marble, the exquisite ornamentation, precious gemstones used and its picturesque location, all make a visit to the Taj Mahal gain a place amongst the most sought-after tours in the world.

However, until you know the love story behind the construction of the Taj Mahal, the beauty of the same would not enliven in your heart and mind and instead would come up as just another beautiful building/monument.

It is the love behind this outstanding monument that has given a life to this monument. Come and explore the visceral charisma that it emanates!

## THE RED FORT OF DELHI

The Red Fort of Delhi was built by the great Mughal emperor Shah Jahan. The Red Fort or the Lal Qila is located in the heart of Old Delhi and was previously known as Qila-e-Mu'alla of the then Shahjanabad, Shah Jahan's new capital.

Construction of Delhi Red Fort started in 1639 and within a span of 9 years, the colossal structure was built. It took more that 10 million rupees during the reign of Shah Jahan to create this structure in red sandstone.

As you enter the Red Fort today, you will find a group of trained guides leaping towards you to adorn in a typically Indian manner to offer their cordiality.

You will definitely discover a haven of peace inside the fort after you leave the frantic streets of Old Delhi.

Like most Islamic buildings in India, the Red Fort is octagonal in shape. The Red Fort is 900 meter by 550 meter. The height of its tower is about 33.5 meters.

Towards the north, you will find Salimgarh fort. A moat lays outside the Red fort which was previously connected with the Yamuna River. The Red Fort is in fact a daunting structure.

The Red Fort has some major attractions inside the fort. They are as follows:

Mumtaz Mahal

The Rang Mahal

The Khas Mahal

The Diwan-i-Am

The Diwan-i-Khas

The Hamam

The Shah Burj

On 15th of August every year the National Flag of India is hoisted at the Red Fort by the Prime Minister, celebrating India's independence.

## QUTB-MINAR

Qutb-Minar in red and buff standstone is the highest tower in India. It has a diameter of 14.32 m at the base and about 2.75 m on the top with a height of 72.5 m.

Qutbu'd-Din Aibak laid the foundation of Minar in AD 1199 for the use of the mu'azzin (crier) to give calls for prayer and raised the first storey, to which were added three more storeys by his successor and son-in-law, Shamsu'd-Din Iltutmish (AD 1211-36).

All the storeys are surrounded by a projected balcony encircling the minar and supported by stone brackets, which are decorated with honey-comb design, more conspicuously in the first storey.

Numerous inscriptions in Arabic and Nagari characters in different places of the minar reveal the history of Qutb.

Quwwat-ul-Islam Mosque, to the north-east of minar was built by Qutbu'd-Din Aibak in AD 1198. It is the earliest extant mosque built by the Delhi Sultans.

It consists of a rectangular courtyard enclosed by cloisters, erected with the carved columns and architectural members of 27 Hindu and Jaina temples which were demolished by Qutbu'd-Din Aibak as recorded in his inscription on the main eastern entrance.

The Iron Pillar in the courtyard bears an inscription in Sanskrit in Brahmi script of fourth century AD, according to which the pillar was set up as a Vishnudhvaja (standard of god Vishnu) on the hill known as Vishnupada in memory of a mighty king named Chandra.

The tomb of Iltutmish (AD 1211-36) was built in AD 1235. It is a plain square chamber of red sandstone, profusely carved with inscriptions, geometrical and arabesque patterns in Saracenic tradition on the entrances and the whole of interior.

Ala'i-Darwaza, the southern gateway of the Quwwat-ul-Islam mosque was constructed by Alau'd-Din Khalji in AH 710 (AD 1311) as recorded in the inscriptions engraved on it.

Ala'i Minar which stands to the north of Qutb-Minar, was commenced by Alau'd-Din Khalji, with the intention of making it twice the size of earlier Minar.

## RAJ GHAT

Raj Ghat, the cremation site of Mahatma Gandhi is one of the most visited sites in Delhi. It consists of a simple square black-marble platform that stands on the spot where Mahatma Gandhi was cremated.

Nearby, there are cremation sites of Jawaharlal Nehru - the first Prime Minister of India, Indira Gandhi, Sanjay Gandhi, Rajiv Gandhi and Lal Bahadur Shastri.

Raj Ghat is situated to the south of Red Fort and is very peaceful. The black marble tomb is inscribed by the words 'Hey Ram!', the last words that were spoken by Mahatma Gandhi, as he fell down after being shot by Nathuram Godse.

The whole edifice of the Samadhi reflects the simple and nature-loving personality of the great leader. The cenotaph stands surrounded by earthworks that protect it from the flooding of the Yamuna.

It is customary to circumambulate the tomb three times. The powerful spiritual aura of the place touches one's heart. This national shrine has an eternal flame and the sandstone walls enclosing it are inscribed with various passages written by Gandhi.

The entire area of Rajghat stands surrounded by trees and here, one can see some of the most exotic shrubs of the country.

It is known by the name of Rajghat Samadhi Committee and was created by an Act of Parliament in 1951.

Vijay Ghat is the memorial of Prime Minister Lal Bhadur Shastri, while Indira Gandhi was cremated in Shakti Sthal.

Rajeev Gandhi followed his mother's footsteps and was the most beloved Prime Minister of India, when he was slaughtered in a terrorist attack. He was cremated at the Veer Bhoomi.

# LETTERS

***WRITE AN APPLICATION TO YOUR PRINCIPAL TO ALLOW YOU FREE SCHOOL UNIFORM.***

To

The Principal,

G.D. Soni Sr. Sec. School,

Pusa Road,

New Delhi

Sir,

Most respectfully I beg to say that I am a student of VI A class in your school. My father had met with an accident last Sunday. Doctors have advised him to take complete bed rest for six months. He is a private servant.

Now he cannot afford my expenditure on uniform. I have been very good at my studies and secured 85% marks in the final examination.

Kindly allow me to have free school uniform.

Thanking you,

Your faithfully,

Sudeep

VI-A

19th April, 20__

***WRITE AN APPLICATION TO YOUR SCOUT MASTER FOR ENROLMENT AS A SCOUT.***

To

The Scout Master,
Ramjas Sen. Sec. School,
Pusa Road,
New Delhi.

Sir,

Respectfully, I request you to enrol me as a scout. I am interested in scouting very much. I know first-aid also. My mother is a doctor. I have learnt first-aid from him. I hope you would give me a chance.

Thanking you,

Yours faithfully,

Rajeev Kumar

VI-C

15th Nov., 20...........

## *INVITATION TO DIWALI CELEBRATIONS*

G-15, Rani Bagh,
New Delhi

25th October, 20___

Dear Sudeep,

Diwali is not far off and already our colony resounds with crackers in the night. I am so excited that I've already exhausted my stock of 'anars', 'dhani' and other big bombs. If there were a terrorist, I could blow him up.

A uncle of mine is contributing 500 rupees for our Diwali crackers and sweets this time. It's going to be great fun. Could you come and join the fun? Please do.

Your loving friend,
Praveen

## *CONGRATULATIONS ON THE BIRTHDAY*

1/20, Gulabi Bagh,

New Delhi

October 5, 20____

My dear Joni,

My congratulations to you on your 12th birthday on

26th April, 20__. May God give you strength and happiness and a long life.

We are sending you your dear carromboard and a few books. Do write how you liked the gifts? Asha didi also sends you her congratulations at the occasion.

Yours sincerely,

Sudeep

### *LETTER OF CONGRATULATIONS ON GETTING A SCHOLARSHIP*

85, Moti Nagar,

New Delhi

12th March 20__

Dear Ashok,

Congratulations for winning the British Council Scholarship for studies in Library Science in the UK. Your studies abroad will enhance your curriculum vitae when looking for a job.

England can be cold even in March and so take warm clothing. Once you're there you'll need a mackintosh since it rains always.

Yours sincerely,

Yogesh

## *WRITE AN APPLICATION TO YOUR PRINCIPAL REQUESTING HIM TO ARRANGE SPECIAL COACHING CLASSES OF ENGLISH AND MATHEMATICS.*

To

The Principal,

Delhi Public School,

New Delhi

Sir,

I beg to say that I am a student of class VI-A. I bring to your kind notice that our courses in maths and English have not so far been fully covered.

Our maths teacher was on leave for quite a long time. Our English teacher was busy in school accounts. Thus our studies have suffered.

I, therefore, request you to arrange special coaching classes as soon as possible.

Thanking you,

Yours faithfully,

Sandhya Singh

VI A

19 Dec., 20___

## *LETTER TO YOUR PRINCIPAL EXPLAINING WHY YOU WEREABSENT FROM SCHOOL.*

To

The Principal,
Ramjas Public School,
Raja Garden,
New Delhi

Sir,

I am very sorry to state that I could not be present in my class on 17th and 18th November. My father was out of station, and my mother suddenly developed high fever.

There was none else to look after her. I was not in a position to inform about it earlier. Therefore, kindly grant me leave for the above two days.

Thanking you,

Yours faithfully,
Rohit Sharma
Class VI-A
19 Dec., 20__

## *WRITE AN APPLICATION TO YOUR PRINCIPAL FOR SICK LEAVE.*

To

The Principal,
Govt. Boys Sen. Sec. School,
Najafgarh,
New Delhi

Sir,

Respectfully I beg to say that I am a student of class VI-A. I have been suffering from fever since yesterday. My doctor has advised me rest for two days. So I cannot attend the school.

Kindly grant me leave from 12-09-20___ to 13-09-20___. I shall be very grateful to you.

Thanking you,

Your obediently,
Pankaj Bansal
VI-A
12th Sep., 20___

### *WRITE AN APPLICATION TO THE PRINCIPAL OF YOUR SCHOOL FOR A CHARACTER CERTIFICATE.*

To

The Principal,
Arya Public School,
Janak Puri, New Delhi

Sir,

I am student of V class in your school. Now I am seeking admission in a government school in Gulabi Bagh, as we have recently shifted there.

My father has bought his own house there. Here, we were living with my grand parents. Since I have to submit a character certificate in the new school, issue me the same.

Thanking you,

Yours obediently,
Ragini Verma
V A
5th April, 20__

## *WRITE AN APPLICATION TO THE PRINCIPAL FOR LEAVE FOR AN URGENT PIECE OF WORK.*

To

The Principal,

Modern Sen. Sec. School,

Anand Vihar,

New Delhi

Sir,

I beg to say that I have an urgent piece of work at home. So, I cannot attend my school today.

Kindly grant me leave for today.

Thanking you,

Yours faithfully,

Vinod Khanna

V-A

17th April, 20____

### *A LETTER TO THE CAPTAIN OF ANOTHER SCHOOL CRICKET TEAM FOR A FRIENDLY MATCH.*

To,

The Captain,

Cricket Team,

D.A.V. Sen. Secondary School,

Pusa Road,

New Delhi.

Dear Sir,

Our school cricket team would like to play friendly 20-20 match with your team. We would like to play the match on December 10, 20__ at 1 P.M. at our school ground . We can change the date by two or three days if you like.

Kindly let me know if you accept our request.

Yours truly,
Rakesh Kumar
Captain
Cricket team,
Ramjas Govt. Boys' Sr. Sec. School
Faridabad
November 25th, 20.......

***LETTER OF SYMPATHY ON THEFT***

25/5, Ashok Vihar

New Delhi

3rd Nov. 20__

Dear Ramesh,

I am taken aback to learn through this morning's newspaper that the burglars broke into your house last night and made away with cash and jewellery worth Rupees One Lakh.

I'm sure the police must be doing its best to trace the thieves and the culprits shall not be allowed to escape. In the meantime, if I can be of any service to you, please do let me know immediately.

Your faithfully,

Satish Kumar

***LETTER OF SYMPATHY ON MEETING WITH AN ACCIDENT***

403/21, Tilak Nagar,

New Delhi

3rd Nov. 20___

Dear Arun,

Rakesh has just given me the news that your cycle

crashed with a scooter last night and that you sustained minor injuries in your hands and knees. Thank God, the injuries are minor ones and you can take the Annual Exams.

In future, drive carefully.

Your loving friend,

Arun Kumar

***LETTER TO YOUR FRIEND ASKING HIM TO VISIT THE HILL STATION DURING, SUMMER VACATIONS.***

B-3/16, Ranjeet Nagar,

New Delhi

12th Nov. 20___.

My dear Rajeev,

I received your letter yesterday. I was glad to know that you have passed your VI class vacations on 15th May.

My father has made a programme to take us to Shimla. We will stay there for 15 days. Please join us. Yours will be a nice company.

Remember, I won't like to have a reply in the negative. It will be great disappoint to me if you don't come.

Do bring your camera also.

Yours sincerely,

Ravi

## ***WRITE A LETTER TO YOUR FRIEND INVITING HIM TO YOUR BROTHER'S MARRIAGE.***

240, Tilak Nagar

New Delhi.

25th Nov. 20__

My dear Alok,

You will be glad to know that my brother's marriage is taking place on 25th Nov. My brother has asked me to invite you.

So you are cordially invited to attend the marriage. You are requested to come two or three days before the marriage to help us in preparations.

Please convey my best regards to your parents and love to youngers.

Yours sincerely,

Mukesh Mehra

## *LETTER OF CONDOLENCE TO A FRIEND ON THE DEATH OF HIS MOTHER*

53, Roop Nagar,

New Delhi

23rd Nov. 20__

Dear Ravi,

I was very shocked when I heard the sad news of your mother's death. My sympathy is with you in this sad movement.

May God grant peace to the departed soul and give you courage to bear the loss!

Sincerely,

Manish Kumar Verma

## *LETTER OF THANKS FOR AN INVITATION TO EXHIBITION*

35/C, Ranjeet Nagar,
New Delhi.
Nov. 22nd, 20___
Dear Sandhya,

Thank you for your Special Invitation for your paintings on Rajasthan displayed at Green Art Gallery, R.K. Puram.

It was indeed a privilege to visit the exhibition and view your oil paintings. We wish you all the success and many more such exhibitions.

With regards.

Yours sincerely,

Renu Sharma

### *LETTER TO YOUR FRIEND INVITING HIM TO YOUR SISTER'S WEDDING.*

405/14, Avantika,
Rohini, Sector-8,
New Delhi

25th April, 20__

Dear Gagan,

I am very happy to inform you that my sister Rekha is getting married on 9th May, 20__. The marriage party will come from Mumbai. The marriage ceremony will be held at our residence.

Please give us the pleasure of your company on this auspicious occasion. Herein is enclosed the invitation card.

Thanking you,

Yours sincerely,

Rohit Sharma

***REPLY ABOVE.***

5/25, Ran Das Colony,

Faridabad

29th April, 20__

Dear Rohit,

Thank you for your invitation on your sister's wedding. But I have a problem. 9th May falls on Sunday and I am going to Punjab to attend the marriage of my uncle. I am sorry, I will not be able to attend your sister's marriage.

I hope you will try and understand my problem and excuse me for my absence.

Thanking you,

Yours sincerely,

Gagan Jain

## *LETTER TO YOUR FRIEND INVITING HIM TO CELEBRATE NEW YEAR WITH YOU.*

24, Shastri Nagar,
New Delhi
2nd Dec., 20__

My Dear Rohit,

Bang-Bang! Yes this is the time to rejoice. It is time to say good-bye to 20___ and welcome the new year. We are planning to enter the new year with a big bang.

We have planned to celebrate the new year by having a party in our garden. Yes, it will be mid-night and chilly cold. For this we will have a big bon-fire. Around this, we will be playing and dancing, singing, drinking and eating.

I hope you won't fail to come.

Regards to your parents.

Yours sincerely,
Gagan Jain

## *REPLY ACCEPTING THE ABOVE INVITATION.*

4/14, Padam Singh Colony,
New Delhi

16th Dec., 20___

My Dear Gagan,

I was glad to receive your letter. How can I miss the party? I am very thankful to you for the invitation. I will come earlier on that day. It will be a great joy to meet all the friends.

Yours sincerely,

Rohit Verma

***REPLY REFUSING THE ABOVE INVITATION.***

4/14, Padam Singh Colony,

New Delhi

16th Dec., 20___

My Dear Gagan,

I was glad to receive your kind letter. I am sorry to inform you that I am not in a position to attend the party. My mother is seriously ill. I attend on him day and night. I am really unlucky to miss such a happy company.

Yours sincerely,

Rohit Verma

## *WRITE A LETTER TO YOUR FRIEND INVITING HIM FOR YOUR BIRTHDAY PARTY.*

1166, Rama Colony,

Faridabad (Hr.)

5th Nov., 20__

My dear Rekha,

You will be glad to know that my birthday falls on 19th of November. I shall celebrate the day at my residence. There will be a grand party.

I have invited our common friends, Renu, Anita, Manju and Mamta. I hope you would enjoy their company.

In the evening, we shall go to see a new movie. The next day, I shall take you around Faridabad. You will be able to see many industrial plants and Badkal lake.

You will certainly enjoy your visit.

I am looking forward to your arrival.

With regards,

Sandhya Singh

## *WRITE A LETTER TO YOUR FRIEND CONGRATULATING HIM ON HIS BRILLIANT SUCCESS.*

4/24A, R. K. Puram,

New Delhi

16th Nov., 20__.

Dear Rahul,

I am very happy to know that you have secured eighty per cent marks in your final examination. I most heartily congratulate you on your grand success.

I am proud of you. My parents are also very happy to hear of your grand success. Your success is really remarkable.

You worked hard. You did not waste your time. You avoided bad company. I am happy over it. Your parents and teachers must be feeling proud of you.

When are you coming here ? We will celebrate your success on your arrival.

I wish you luck in times to come.

Yours sincerely,

Arjun Rawat

## *WRITE A LETTER TO YOUR FRIEND INVITING HIM TO SPEND A SUNDAY WITH YOU*

25/2, Jain Colony,
Pusa Road,
New Delhi.

25th Nov. 20___

My dear Ashok,

It is long since you paid us a visit. My elder brother is coming from Dehradun on Sunday the 30th November. He will be here for a week. You know how he loves you.

I shall be very happy if you can come down to us on 7th of next month. It is Sunday on that day and you are free. We all three shall gossip, eat and enjoy.

Confirm your coming by the immediate reply and please don't say no.

Please convey my best regards to your parents and love to youngers.

Waiting hopely,

Yours lovingly,

Ankit Sharma

## *LETTER TO FRIEND ON HIS FAILURE TO PASS THE EXAMINATION*

405A, Mahavir Vatica,
Karol Bagh,
New Delhi.

25th Dec. 20___

Dear Amit,

It is a matter of no small sorrow to me to learn from your brother that you failed this year in the Intermediate examination. I sympathise with you in your great misfortune.

But dear friend, don't lose heart, remember that failures are the pillars of success. Forget the past and take care of the future.

May be, the next year you would pass examination with good division. With kinds regards to your parents and love to Rakha and Golu.

Yours affectionately,

Pradeep

***REPLY***

51C, Suraj Colony,
Faridabad
30th Dec. 20___

Dear Pradeep,

It is very difficult the grief that I and my parents felt at the shocking news of my failure but your kind letter, containing some nice pieces of advice, filled me with hope and courage and I am sure to succeed next time with good division.

Thanks for your sympathy,

Yours,
Amit Gupta

## *WRITE A LETTER TO THE S.H.O. OF YOUR AREA REPORTING A THEFT IN YOUR HOUSE.*

C-45, Rama Vihar,
New Delhi
23rd, Nov. 20___

To
The S.H.O,
Police Station,
Rama Vihar,
Delhi

Sir,

I beg to report the theft of my cycle on 25th November, 20___. I had gone to the market to purchase books. I locked my cycle outside and went in. I came back after ten minutes.

My cycle was stolen. It is a Hero cycle. It is new cycle. Its number is DC-2052. Kindly register the report and look into the matter.

Yours faithfully,
Harish Kumar

## *WRITE A LETTER TO A BOOKSELLER ORDERING BOOK.*

25, Ganesh Colony,

Faridabad,

25th Nov. 20___

To,

M/s. Modern Book Distributors,

Educational Publishers,

Bhola Nath Nagar,

Shahdara,

Delhi

Dear Sirs,

Please send me the following books per V.P.P at your earliest convenience. Kindly send the latest editions of these books.

(1) The Dictionary of English. 1 copy

(2) English Essays and Letters. 1 copy

(3) English Reader VI Class 1 copy

(4) Idioms and Phrases 1 copy

(5) Stories book for 3rd class 1 copy

(6) Science book for 3rd class 1 copy

(7) Modern Book of Essays 1 copy

(8) Dictionary of Idioms 1 copy

(9) Dictionary of Proverbs 1 copy

(10) Gems of Quotations 1 copy

(11) Big book of great speeches 1 copy

Thanking you,

Yours truly,

Kamal Aggarwal

***WRITE A LETTER TO A SPORTS GOODS OR MANUFACTURER TO SEND YOU SOME SPORTS MATERIAL.***

548, Inderlok,

New Delhi

24th Dec., 20__

To,

M/s Goodwin Sports,

Ashoka Road,

New Delhi

Dear Sirs,

Kindly supply the following articles of sports in good condition. Mention the specification in your bill.

| | | |
|---|---|---|
| (1) | Badminton Racquet | 10 pcs. |
| (2) | Badminton Nets | 2 pcs. |
| (3) | Shuttle-Cocks | 2 dozen |
| (4) | Volleyball laceless | 6 pcs. |
| (5) | Cricket Bats | 6 pcs. |
| (6) | Cricket Balls | 10 pcs. |

Please supply the material to the above address within a week. The payment will be made a cash.

Thanking you,

Yours faithfully,

Vijay Kumar

## *WRITE A LETTER TO THE POST MASTER COMPLAINING AGAINST THE IRREGULAR DELIVERY OF YOUR LETTERS.*

258, Tilak Nagar,

New Delhi

Nov. 25, 20__

To,

The Post Master,

G.P.O. Kashmeri Gate,

New Delhi

Sir,

I am very sorry to report that my letters are not properly delivered to me.

The postman of our area, Shri Sunil Pal, is very irregular and careless. He does not perform his duty honestly. He delivered my letters either to wrong persons or to children playing in the street.

On the outer wall of my house I have put up a letter box bearing my name and address. But he does not put my letters into my house. I requested him many times but it no effect. I am, therefore, obliged to complain to you against him.

Please take necessary action. I shall feel highly obliged to you for this.

Yours faithfully,

Sudeep Kumar

## *WRITE A LETTER TO YOUR FATHER ABOUT YOUR POOR PERFORMANCE IN THE SCHOOL TEST.*

Gandhi Hostel,

Mumbai

12th Nov., 20__

Dear father,

I am sorry to inform you that I could not do better in the last test. The reason is that I am weak in English and maths. I also remained sick for a week. I promise I would improve in the annual examinations. I assure you that I have changed my ways. I am now working hard.

I complete my home-task regularly. I have now joined extra classes also. I also study for three hours at home. I will be active in future and satisfy my all teachers. You can write to any of them.

Once again I assure you that I will come up to your expectations.

With regards to mother and love to youngers.

Yours affectionately,

Rahul Gupta

***WRITE A LETTER TO FATHER TO INCREASE POCKET-ALLOWANCE.***

25, Chandan Nagar,
Boys Hostel,
Dehradun
April 25, 20__
Respected father,

I am quite well here and hope all will be well there too. My examination is coming near and I am burning midnight oil to get first division.

Papa, for some time I have been short of money every month. I purchased some necessary books last month. The money sent by you does not last for a full month. Reason, you know well.

Prices are up. Please increase my pocket money. I also know your limitations but Papa it is a matter of three months only.

Convey my regards to dear Mother and love to Ravi.

Yours loving son,
Rahul

## *A LETTER TO FATHER REQUESTING FOR MONEY FOR THE PURCHASE OF BOOKS.*

24, D.A.V. Hostel,

New Delhi,

Dec. 4, 20........

Dear Father,

You will be glad to know that I am doing well in the school. I do my work regularly. Our S.Science teacher has asked us to purchase a new book of Kundra Bawa . I also want to purchase a dictionary for my personal use. I need money to purchase a pair of shoes. Please send me Rs. 1500/- money order.

Pay my respects to dear mother and love to Rosy.

You loving son,

Rakesh Kumar

VI A

## *WRITE A LETTER TO YOUR FATHER GIVING HIM HOME NEWS AND ASKING FOR MONEY.*

4/14C, Ramjas Chowk,

New Delhi,

Nov. 4, 20..........

Dear Father,

I got your letter this morning. There is a bad news for you. Mother has been ill since Sunday last. We have spent a lot of money on medicines. Now she is recovering slowly. Asha goes to school regularly and studies at home. I have not paid her school fee. The money you set last month has been spent out.

Kindly send more money this time.

Yours affectionately,

Rohit

## *WRITE AN APPLICATION TO THE PRINCIPAL OF YOUR SCHOOL FOR A SCHOOL LEAVING CERTIFICATE.*

To

The Principal,

Golden Public School,

New Delhi

Sir,

Respectfully, I beg to say that my father is a government servant. He has been transferred to Mumbai. So, I cannot continue my study here.

I, therefore, request you to issue me a school leaving certificate so that I may join the new school there.

Thanking you,

Yours obediently,

Rakesh Kumar,

Class VI-A

25th April, 20__

***WRITE AN APPLICATION TO THE PRINCIPAL OF YOUR SCHOOL ASKING FOR TWO DAYS LEAVE FOR YOUR BROTHER'S MARRIAGE.***

To

The principal,
New Era Sr. Sec. School,
Rohini, Sector-8,
Delhi

Sir.

Respectfully, I beg to say that the marriage of my brother is taking place on 23th April.

The marriage will take place in our native village in Haryana. I have to make preparations for the marriage.

Kindly grant me leave for two days from 22nd April to 24th.

Thanking you,

Yours obediently,
Rekha Sharma
VIth-A
22nd April, 20____

## *WRITE AN APPLICATION TO YOUR PRINCIPAL FOR CHANGE OF YOUR SUBJECTS.*

To

The Principal,
Akash International Public School,
Vikas Puri,
New Delhi

Sir,

Respectfully I beg to say that I chose science as my subject in the English medium on the advice of my friend. But now I find that my English is weak. So I want to change from English to Hindi medium.

Kindly allow me to change this.

Thanking you,

Yours obediently,
Sanjay Shukla
VI-A
23rd Nov. 20___

## *WRITE AN APPLICATION TO YOUR PRINCIPAL FOR REMISSION OF FINE.*

To

The Principal,
Govt. Model School,
New Delhi

Sir,

Respectfully I beg say that I am a student of class VI-A. Yesterday while on way to the school my bus broke down and I reached late. My class teacher got angry and imposed a fine of Rs. 10/- on me.

I am very good student. My father is a poor man. He cannot pay the fine. I, therefore, request you to remit my fine. I shall be thankful to you for this kindness.

Thanking you,

Yours faithfully,
Deepak Rawat
VI-A

10th Dec., 20___

## *WRITE AN APPLICATION TO YOUR PRINCIPAL REQUESTING HIM TO ALLOW YOU TO CHANGE YOUR SECTION.*

To

The Principal,
Delhi Public School,
Uttam Nagar,
New Delhi

Sir,

Respectfully I beg to say that I am a student of VI-A. I want to change my section from A to B because my cousin, Mukul Jain, is in class VI-B. Ours is a joint family, and we study together and have many books in common.

Kindly allow me to change my section and oblige.

Thanking you,

Yours obediently
Akash Jain
VI-A
25th May, 20__

### *WRITE AN APPLICATION TO YOUR PRINCIPAL REQUESTING HIM TO GRANT YOU FULL FEE CONCESSION.*

To

The Principal,
G.D. Soni Govt. Girls' Sen. Sec. School,
Pusa Road,
New Delhi

Sir,

Respectfully I beg to say that I am a student of class VI-B of your school. My father is in private service. He gets Rs. 4500 per month all told. I have one brother and two sisters. They are also studying in another school.

He finds it difficult to pay full fees for all the three of us. I have been very good at my studies and secured 87% marks in the final examination.

Kindly grant me full fee concession for which I shall be obliged to you.

Thanking you,

Yours obediently,
Kamal Aggarwal
VI-B
22nd April, 20__